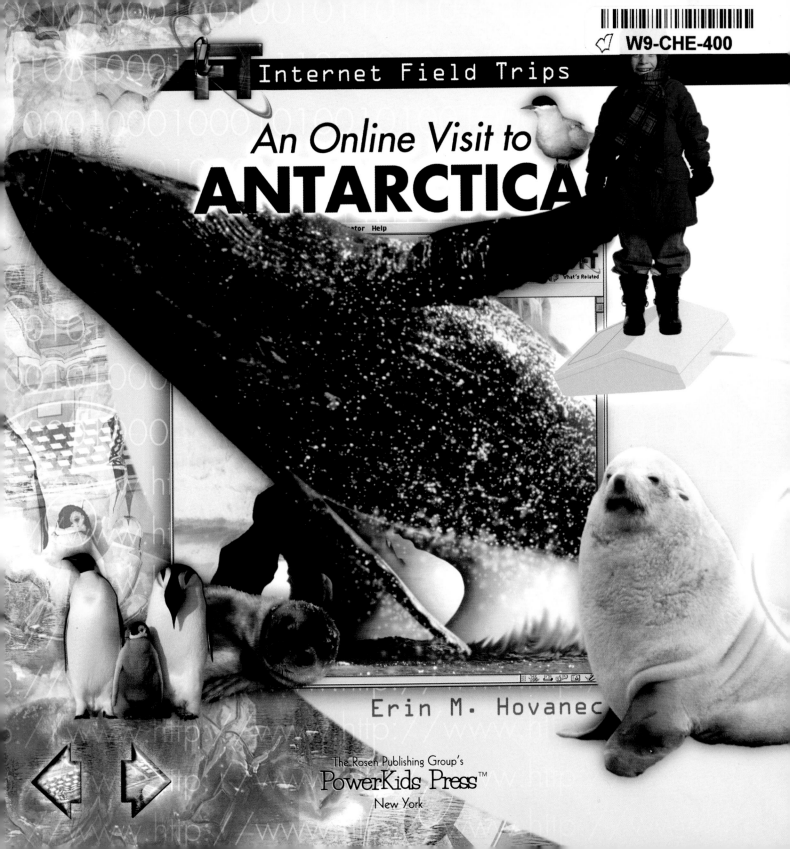

Internet Field Trips

An Online Visit to
ANTARCTICA

Erin M. Hovanec

The Rosen Publishing Group's
PowerKids Press™
New York

For my brother, Chris Hovanec

Published in 2001 by The Rosen Publishing Group, Inc.
29 East 21st Street, New York, NY 10010
Copyright © 2001 by The Rosen Publishing Group, Inc.

First Edition

Book Design: Maria Melendez

Photo Credits: Cover, title page, (whale) © Ron Sanford/International Stock; title page, (penquins, baby seal, tern) © Digital Stock; title page, (tunnel through iceberg) © Christiana Carvalho/Frank Lane Picture Agency/CORBIS; title page, (Antarctic fur seal) © Fritz Polking/Frank Lane Picture Agency/CORBIS; p. 19 (Roald Amundsen) © CORBIS; p. 11 (plant fossils), 16 (krill) © Peter Johnson/CORBIS; p. 20 (scientist at work) © 1984 by Michele & Tom Grimm/International Stock; p. 8 (Laguna San Rafael glaciers) © Peter Langone/International Stock; p. 7 (snow covered mountain) © Ronn Maratea/International Stock; p. 15 (Killer Whale) © Ron Sanford/International Stock; p.12 (Mount Erebus) © Miwako Ikeda/International Stock.

Hovanec, Erin M.
    An online visit to Antarctica / Erin M. Hovanec.
        p. cm.— (Internet field trips)
    Includes index.
    Summary: An online trip to various internet web sites reveals a variety of facts about the continent of Antarctica, the continent which covers the South Pole, the most southern point on earth.
    ISBN 0-8239-5656-3
    1. Antarctica—Computer network resources—Juvenile literature. 2. Antarctica—Computer network resources—Directories—Juvenile literature. 3. Web sites—Directories—Juvenile literature. 4. World wide web—Juvenile literature. [1. Antarctica.] I. Title. II. Series.

G863 .H68 2000
025.06'91989—dc21   00-039161

Manufactured in the United States of America.

Contents

Let's Get Started

You can surf the Net from a computer from home, or you can use a computer at your school or public library to get online. Here's what you'll need to use the Internet.

A personal computer
You'll need a personal computer with a monitor, or screen, a mouse, and a keyboard.

A modem
Your computer must also have a modem, which is a device that links it to the telephone line.

A telephone connection
You need this to connect your modem to other computers.

Internet software
You use Internet software, such as a search engine, to help tell your computer how to use the Internet.

An Internet Service Provider
The modem will connect you to an Internet Service Provider (ISP). ISPs allow you to get on the Internet for a small monthly fee.

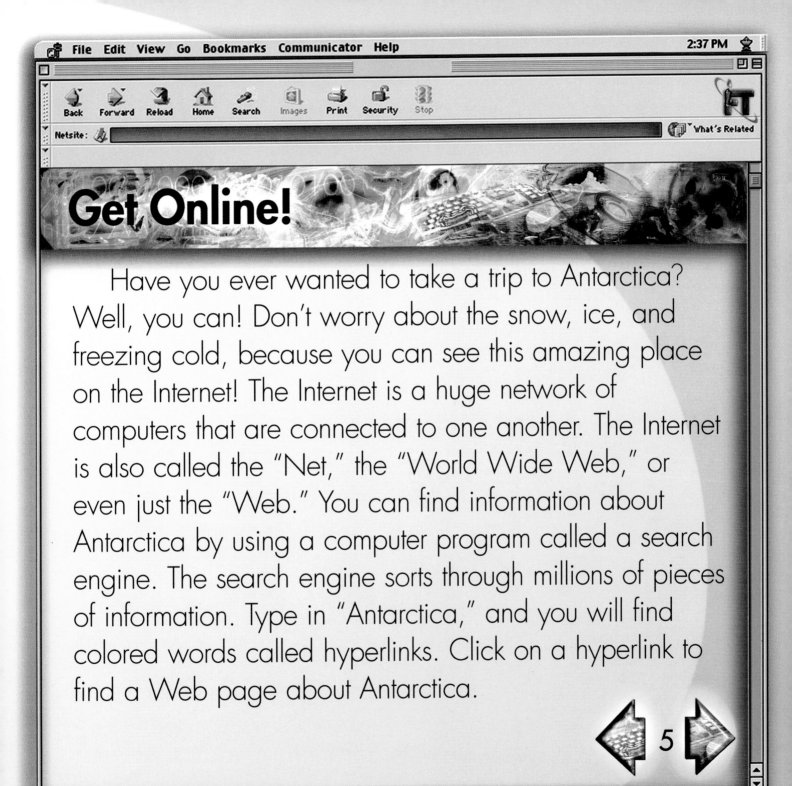

Back   Forward   Reload   Home   Search   Images   Print   Security   Stop

Netsite: What's Related

Get Online!

Have you ever wanted to take a trip to Antarctica? Well, you can! Don't worry about the snow, ice, and freezing cold, because you can see this amazing place on the Internet! The Internet is a huge network of computers that are connected to one another. The Internet is also called the "Net," the "World Wide Web," or even just the "Web." You can find information about Antarctica by using a computer program called a search engine. The search engine sorts through millions of pieces of information. Type in "Antarctica," and you will find colored words called hyperlinks. Click on a hyperlink to find a Web page about Antarctica.

5

Search for the End
of the Earth

Antarctica is perhaps the most mysterious of Earth's seven **continents**. It lies at the southern tip of the globe. The continent covers the **South Pole**, the most southern point on Earth. The southern parts of the Atlantic, Pacific, and Indian Oceans combine to form the Antarctic Ocean. The cold, stormy waters of the Antarctic Ocean surround Antarctica. At 5.4 million square miles (14 million sq km), Antarctica is the fifth-largest continent. Most of this continent is made up of the Antarctic **ice cap**, a layer of snow and ice 6,500 feet (1,981 m) thick that covers the land. Without the ice cap, Antarctica would actually be the smallest of the seven continents.

6

Antarctica has beautiful glaciers. Glaciers are very slow-moving masses of ice.

Learn more about Antarctica:
http://www.pbs.org/wnet/nature/antarctica/index.html
http://www.ozemail.com.au/~reed/hot/map.html

To learn more about the weather in Antarctica:
http://www.nbs.ca.uk/public/icd/wmc/Blueice/weather.html
http://www.terraquest.com/va/index.html

A Cold, Cold Climate

If you like cold weather, you'll love Antarctica! Antarctica is the coldest place on Earth. It rarely gets warmer than 32 degrees Fahrenheit (0° C) there. The coldest temperature, -129° degrees Fahrenheit (-89° C), was recorded in Antarctica. Thick, heavy snow falls along Antarctica's coast, but very little rain or snow falls in its center. Winds can reach up to 150 miles per hour (241 km) and create dangerous snowstorms. The winds blow so much snow around that it becomes impossible to see anything at all. These storms are called "white outs." Antarctica has six months of constant darkness and six months where it is always daylight.

The snow, ice, and mist on this mountain in Antarctica show why this continent is the coldest place on Earth.

9

The Antarctic Ice Cap

You may find it hard to believe, but Antarctica wasn't always cold and icy. Scientists have discovered **fossils** of plants, dinosaurs, and other animals that lived millions of years ago on the once warm and green continent. About 25 to 37 million years ago, **glaciers** began to form around the South Pole. For the last five million years, Antarctica has been buried under an icy surface. The ice cap covers about 98 percent of Antarctica. In its deepest places, it's about 10 times higher than the tallest buildings in the world! This ice cap could be the largest body of fresh water on Earth. If the ice cap were to melt, the oceans would rise and flood cities around the globe.

These plant fossils were found in the Antarctic ice. Scientists believe they are millions of years old. ▶

For more information about the Antarctic ice cap and glaciers:
http://www.secretsoftheice.org
http://www.glacier.rice.edu/
http://www.awi-bremerhaven.de/Eistour/index-e.htmlh

To learn more about Antarctica's geography:
http://www.pbs.org/wgbh/nova/warnings/
http://kidsinternet.about.com/kids/kidsinternet/library/weekly/

Really Cool Geography

East Antarctica has broad glaciers, steep mountains, and deep valleys. Some of the rocks in this region are over 570 million years old. The center of the region is a **plateau** about 10,000 feet (3,048 m) high. The South Pole is located in this plateau. Strong winds on the plateau create ridges in the snow. These ridges are called sastrugi, and they can be up to 6 feet (1.8 m) high! The Transantarctic Mountains divide the western and eastern regions of the continent. The highest point is on Mount Vinson Massif. West Antarctica also has many volcanoes. Mount Erebus, the continent's most active volcano, lies on Ross Island.

◄ *Broad, flat sheets of ice, called ice shelves, surround Ross Island. Mount Erebus, an active volcano, is on Ross Island.*

◄ 13 ►

Famous Antarctic Animals

Few plants can survive in Antarctica's cold **climate**. Plants such as **lichen** and **mosses** cling to its rocky coasts. The continent's waters are home to many kinds of whales, including blue whales, humpback whales, and killer whales. Blue whales can grow up to 100 feet (30 m) long. Lots of different types of seals spend their days swimming, playing, and sleeping around the Antarctic coast. There are elephant seals, fur seals, and crabeater seals, among others. Antarctica's most famous animals are its many types of penguins. Emperor penguins are the biggest. They grow to be four feet (1.2 m) tall. Penguins can't fly, but they are fast, skillful swimmers.

Killer whales, also known as orcas, travel in packs like wolves. ▶

Learn more about penguins and other Antarctic animals:
http://www.terraquest.com/va/science/science.html
http://www.yourexpedition.com/whale.html

To get more information on Antarctica's ocean creatures:
http://www.antarctic.com.au/encyclopaedia/bio/Bio.html
http://www.yourexpedition.com/birds.html

Life at the Bottom
of the Earth

Over 100 kinds of fish, as well as squid and octopi, live in the Antarctic Ocean. You'll find dolphins and porpoises swimming in its chilly waters, too. Antarctica is also home to many birds, such as albatrosses, cormorants, gulls, and petrels. The most common animals in the Antarctic Ocean are krill, tiny sea creatures that look like shrimp. Krill are the major source of food for many birds, fish, and seals. Some people even eat krill. Swarms of krill gather off the coast of Antarctica during the day. They create a huge red mass in daylight that glows blue-green in color when it becomes dark!

◀ *These shrimplike krill are the main source of food for animals who live in the waters around Antarctica.*

17

Discovering a New Continent

Hundreds of years before the discovery of Antarctica, people dreamed about an unknown continent at the southern tip of Earth. In 1772, James Cook, an English sailor, set sail to find this unknown continent. He traveled far south, but he was unable to sail through the huge blocks of ice and never saw land. Later, explorers discovered islands around Antarctica. In 1821, a Russian sailor named Fabian Bellingshausen was the first person to sail around Antarctica. It wasn't until December 14, 1911, that Roald Amundsen, an explorer from Norway, became the first person ever to reach the South Pole.

18

Roald Amundsen, shown in the small photo, and a team of explorers were the first people to reach the South Pole. ▶

To learn more about Antarctic explorers:
http://www.south-pole.com/p0000017.htm
http://www.terraquest.com/va/history/history.html

For more information on Antarctica:
http://www.terraquest.com/va/ecology/ecology.html
http://www.astro.uchicago.edu/cara/vtour/

Countries Cooperate

Seven countries have laid claim to parts of Antarctica. These countries are Argentina, Australia, Chile, France, Great Britain, New Zealand, and Norway. A map showing the parts that they share would look like the slices of a pizza, with the South Pole in the center. Beginning in 1959, leaders of these and other countries signed the Antarctic **Treaty**. The treaty states that people can use Antarctica only for peaceful reasons, such as scientific research and exploration. Military forces can't enter Antarctica unless they are helping scientists, and all scientific discoveries must be shared with the entire world.

◄ *These scientists are working to protect Antarctica's animals and its environment.*

Back   Forward   Reload   Home   Search   Images   Print   Security   Stop

Netsite: What's Related

Antarctica Today

Antarctica has no native human **population**, or group of people who have been born there. The people who live on the continent are scientists or people who help with scientific research. Few people stay in Antarctica for more than one year. More than 30 countries have scientific stations in Antarctica. The largest American community is at McMurdo Station. During the summer, about 1,300 people live at McMurdo Station. Only 200 people stay for the harsh winter. Scientists there observe animals, record weather, examine glaciers, and study earthquakes. Discoveries made in Antarctica can help people all over the world.

G L O S S A R Y

climate (KLY-mit) The type of weather that a certain area has.

continents (KON-tin-ents) One of the seven great masses of land on Earth.

fossils (FAH-sils) The hardened remains of dead animals and plants that lived long ago.

glaciers (GLAY-sherz) A large mass of ice that very slowly moves down a mountain or along a valley.

ice cap (IYS KAP) A huge layer of ice and snow that covers a large area of land.

lichen (LY-ken) Tiny single-cell plants.

mosses (MOS-es) Very small green plants that usually cover rocks and tree bark.

plateau (plah-TOH) A broad, flat, high mass of land.

population (pop-yoo-LAY-shun) The number of people who live in a region.

South Pole (SAUTH POL) The southernmost point on Earth.

treaty (TREE-tee) A formal agreement, especially one between nations, signed and agreed upon by each nation.

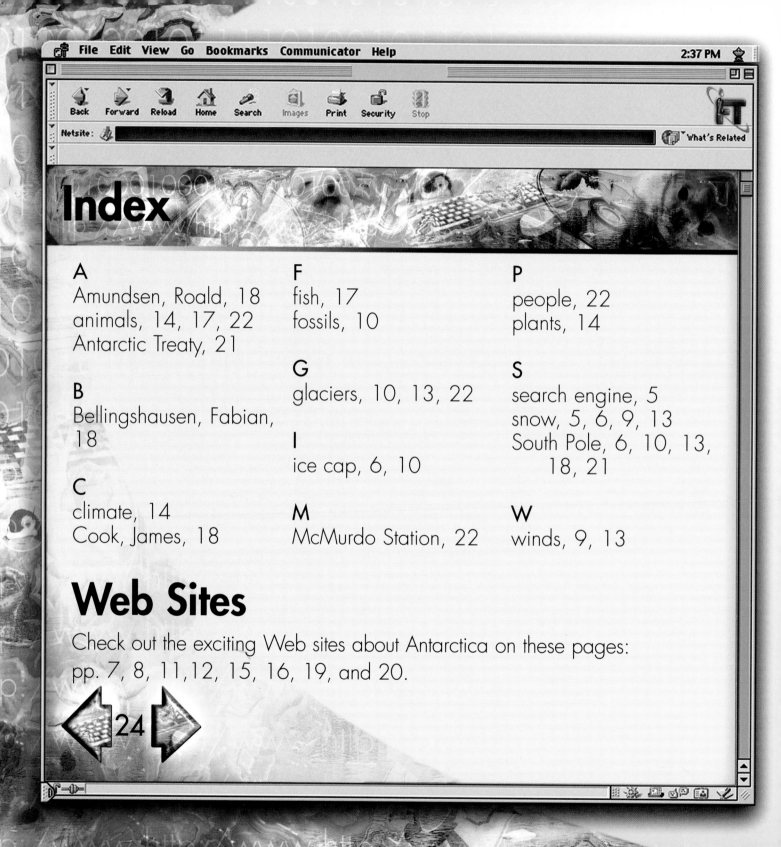

Index

A
Amundsen, Roald, 18
animals, 14, 17, 22
Antarctic Treaty, 21

B
Bellingshausen, Fabian, 18

C
climate, 14
Cook, James, 18

F
fish, 17
fossils, 10

G
glaciers, 10, 13, 22

I
ice cap, 6, 10

M
McMurdo Station, 22

P
people, 22
plants, 14

S
search engine, 5
snow, 5, 6, 9, 13
South Pole, 6, 10, 13, 18, 21

W
winds, 9, 13

Web Sites

Check out the exciting Web sites about Antarctica on these pages:
pp. 7, 8, 11,12, 15, 16, 19, and 20.

24